Winter in the Eye
New & Selected Poems

JOAN McBREEN

salmonpoetry

First Published in 2003 by Salmon Publishing,
Cliffs of Moher, County Clare, Ireland
web: www.salmonpoetry.com
email: info@salmonpoetry.com

Paperback ISBN 1 903392 33 0
Hardback ISBN 1 903392 35 7

A CIP record for this title is available from the British Library.

Cover Artwork: *Winter Garden* by Paddy Lennon, Oil on Canvas
Cover Design & Typesetting: Siobhán Hutson
Printed in Ireland by Colour Books

Salmon Publishing gratefully acknowledges the financial
assistance of The Arts Council/An Chomhairle Ealaíon

the arts
council
an chomhairle
ealaíon

for Jim Carney

By The Same Author

POETRY

The Wind Beyond the Wall. Story Line Press, Oregon, 1990.
Reprinted 1991.

A Walled Garden in Moylough. Story Line Press, Oregon and
Salmon Publishing, Co. Clare, 1995.

AS EDITOR

*The White Page – An Bhileog Bhán: Twentieth-Century Irish
Women Poets*. (Anthology) Salmon Publishing, Co. Clare,
1999, reprinted 2000, 2001.

Acknowledgements

Acknowledgements are due to the editors of the following publications where these poems, or versions of them, first appeared:

Poetry Ireland Review, Irish University Review (Vol.28 No.2), Cyphers, The Honest Ulsterman, Force 10, The Tuam Herald, Or Volge L'Anno – At The Year's Turning (ed. Marco Sonzogni), *The Cork Literary Review* (Vol 8 – ed. Sheila O'Hagan), *Ropes* (Vol 9), *You Can't Eat Flags for Breakfast* (eds. Joseph Sheehy and Joshua Schultz), and *The Clifden Anthology*.

Special thanks to Niall MacMonagle, Eamon Grennan, Billy Collins and Theodore Deppe for invaluable help and encouragement; also to Anne Ward, and to the members of the Galway Writers' Workshop.

The poems taken from *A Walled Garden in Moylough* were published in Ireland by Salmon Publishing and in the U.S.A. by Story Line Press, Brownsville, Oregon. Thanks to editors Jessie Lendennie and Robert McDowell. Also special gratitude to the women poets of Ireland for their support during the years of work on both *The White Page* and on this volume.

The author wishes to include a special thanks to Paddy Lennon, the artist whose painting "Winter Garden" graces the cover of this book.

Author's royalties from this book donated to The Leukaemia Trust, University College Hospital, Galway.

Contents

III. from *A Walled Garden In Moylough*

I.

Winter in the Eye – New Poems

What We Have To Offer

I offer you this near winter's end –
my mother's voice and shooting stars.

In childhood I knew each one
meant a soul in pain or that the dead,
tired of being dead, had come
to astonish some living thing.

Virginia creeper is filled with sunlight
at a railway station, a wind blows in from the sea,
and my mother enters a train
carrying nothing.

I cannot sleep. My mind pictures a road,
my mother walking beside me, singing,
taking me home, turning off the light;
then the night filled with yearning

and my mother's cry: "Look, look up, a shooting star!"

Camellia

"The heart is the toughest part of the body.
Tenderness is in the hands."
     Carolyn Forché

At the winter solstice pink buds
appeared among waxen leaves.
I cupped my hands around them
in sunlight and in snow.

The child's swing, a frozen clothes-line
and bird-table became the silent dead
whose voices and faces
pleaded for attention.

Once, this garden held you,
with your headlong flying from one
to another, whose embraces
were mine of the camellia.

When the buds began to open,
I withdrew
and watched
from my window.

I believed my heart was tough.
The edges of the flowers turned colour,
a deep brown staining each one
until the petals fell.

It is time to name grief,
find words
and bring them to you
with my bare hands.

Cherry-Blossoms

The spring I wondered would you see
comes late. Outside a wood-pigeon's call
and cherry-blossoms lie in drifts
along the edges of the Ballygaddy Road.

Another May, the last one you will spend
at school; the wind still cold in corridors
where others listen to the story
told of you, a story I feared

you might not live to hear,
one I hardly dared believe,
as sunlight falls upon the blossoms
blown across the road and onto the grass.

Sea Bird

Following each other
in an even pattern,
birds fly over the ocean.

From this beach I see one
the wind has taken.

It knows sky, air, water, grass and earth.
A navigator, it flies
to points on its own compass.

Some day, perhaps in early spring
when an inland mist clings
to hedges of white-thorn and yellow whin,

I will see it once more, soaring.

Willows

i.m. Anne Kennedy (1935 – 1998)

> *"No, plant me,*
> *like my Grandmother's blazing dahlias*
> *in the subsuming earth,*
> *where I can be lifted,*
> *where there's a chance of resurrection".*

One day in March you lined up
willow cuttings on your table, stems wrapped
in foil, a gift for each of your friends.

"These will take" you said,
"they will take, I promise,
like no other tree you've ever known."

I placed mine in water
near the light
and waited for the roots to appear.

Even when they did and white fronds
filled the jar, I feared transplanting
my willow into the dark.

In September you left. The first frosts now
lie on the grass and on the willows
whose disconsolate leaves blow around us.

A Cold May

and three seasons
since darkness filled
your house.

The wind blows over Galway
and we no longer draw
warmth from you.

I leave my words
on your wooden tea-trolley
as if they were my gloves.

This room looks out
on Sunday quiet.
Trees are heavy

with leaves
and the book I read
explains neither love nor grief.

Silence Is Not A Space

It is February again. In a distant field
you are a shade under an ash tree.

What would you have me understand when
it is you who constantly returns to disturb me.

On the street you appear in your yellow coat,
your umbrella doing battle with the wind

or you enter a restaurant, smiling, talking loudly
with strangers. I lift the telephone and it
rings out in your empty house.

There is no sense in ordering you like a fiction
to stand next to me.

Instead I see your face behind the daffodils
I carried to you last year on your birthday.
New leaves tremble outside my window
and the spring sun throws shadows into this room.

Silence is the light I see stream across the page.

At Rosses Point

And in Memory Harbour the air
is still and Sunday; sea-gulls
rise and disappear
beyond the waves and little hulls.

And mourning you I feel the sun
warm this chill on Rosses height,
know you are gone and must go on
as I will now and meet the night

and the low, pale light on the land,
the long, long light on the sand.

Solstice 2001

i.m. James Simmons (1933-2001)

Wild roses adorn
the ditches
on the road
from Dunfanaghy
to Falcarragh.

And yesterday
you covered
your father's grave

with armfuls
of fuchsias,
whins and blue–
purple rhododendrons.

Poem in Autumn

Autumn sun gold on the grass,
leaves lie dead in the cold.

The path you walk, once hung
with lilac and laburnum,
is arched over with branches,
stripped and desolate.

These words the wind takes
to the river, words that do not tremble
or weep but scrape the cheek,
burn through the blood,
cold as gulls inland from the sea.

Winter

I

In winter there comes a hush
as if illness had swerved towards us.
We speak of it in quieter tones
believing we can accept harsher weather.

When Gretel decided
they would go together deep into the forest,
she became afraid. Would they lose one another,
would the path disappear?
When she called her brother's name over
and over, he did not come back.

When I look winter in the eye,
I am looking down dense corridors of trees.

II

Sunlight falls on kitchen tiles and chairs,
solidifies worktops, appliances, stacked papers.
Pictures of friends and children
hang on shadowed walls.

I move into this vacancy.

Outside late roses are within reach,
wet leaves clog gutters and drains.

Watching the light flood across the garden
I am startled by a bird beating
its wings against the window-pane.

Like Trees

Some trees bend without breaking
in the harshest of weather;
the willow takes its cue from the air,
its form never the same any moment.

The evening arrives at breakneck speed
and leaves fall on rain-polished paths.
If I walk amongst these yews once more
I want to believe everything happened
as it should, that the night
of darkness was lit by the moon.

The Terminology of Love

Somewhere there is a man weeping
beside a woman he has beaten
and she is thinking about the time
before she allowed him to touch her in love,
when he took the picture of her on the bridge,
her elbows resting on stone,
a basket of windfalls at her feet
and her dress a water-colour blue.

The Bible Garden

for Mark Patrick Hederman

In a year, a decade or a century,
the photographer's presence will be clear.

Here is the picture.

Four people are in the Bible Garden.
Two of them move from plot to plot;
one is naming herbs, plants, vegetables and trees,
sharing each one's symbol and metaphor with the other.

The one with the photographer is near
the farthest edge of the garden wall.

What is said between them is being
listened to intently.

The camera is used only once.

For you this is not enough. You demand more
than the sky darkening or the rain falling,
cooling the hands, faces and necks of those
in the picture.

You want them running from the Bible Garden,
desiring more than they have.

What follows is not easy to say.

Here time has stopped. For some this joy,
for better, for worse, for love of God,
is never enough and this, the world
knows, is the sorrow of the story.

The Wisteria In The Courtyard
Of Dromore House

The wisteria in the courtyard of Dromore House
is yearning towards its own shadow.
Evening. Two women are also yearning
towards one another. One is hiding her face.

It is growing darker. The women leave the courtyard
and enter the house. A moth is shivering over
a candle-flame; small rolls of bread are offered
to the man who appears in the tableau.

His eyes are blue, do you remember?
The women are careful not to look at them,
looking instead at the single branch
of white blossom they carried into the room.

The man is lifting his head; he reaches
for the flowers: "Tell me how long
they last, my dears, how long?"
The moon has lit the courtyard. Music

is playing in the house, the beat insistent.
Candle-light, lamp-light, moonlight…
on the table wine in a stone jug, purple grapes.
Suddenly everyone is older. There is a wind

starting to blow, the door is swept open
and the rest of the story is repeating itself…

The Half-Heard Lament

for Nóirín Ní Riain

Here she is
    running towards me filled with laughter,
    her guinea-fowl scattering to the secret places
    she has made for them. The dress she is wearing
    is lifted by the wind that comes from who knows where.

Then I am
    listening to her murmuring her love to me,
    her voice stitching the words
    of her story together as fishermen stitch
    their nets under the stars.

And her music
    has the sound of frightened birds in it
    and may never be understood; for it too
    comes from some other place as clear
    and cold as the sea.

The Other Side Of The River

The river has its own limits.
You stand on the other side.

I remain where I am,
in the doorway of my house.

Others enter the river first.
From where you are, you call my name.

The world is still.
Figures in the water grow smaller and smaller.

They swim free of nets cast by fishermen
who pull in their catch.

How particular are these things
and none of them mine.

I only once heard your voice.
Stars appear and rain falls.

The river moves on its course,
leaving me to forget myself or learn my place.

Mullaghmore, County Sligo

I

Two at a white table
in front of a hotel –
nothing stirs in the heat of summer;
the smell of sea-wrack.

One points to the children
who wade too far out
without looking back, sun too strong
on their delicate skin.

Only when the two rise
to leave do I hear
their voices
splinter like glass on granite.

II

The wind combs the wild grass
over the strand at Mullaghmore;
beyond the harbour wall
the boats have turned for home.

I think of you waving
near the cliff's edge.
Sea-spray blurs your image,
the warning you call to me

lost in the tumult waves make
on the rocks below.
There is a landscape out there,
somewhere at sea.

Memory

for Medbh McGuckian

There we were in sunlight
our children still young around us,
poetry books in your lap,
you writing your name on them.

These are the memory images,
houses the mind occupies.
These are walls through
which the birds chip
small points of entry.

Tell me, how out of so much
waking and sleeping
came the music of your mind,
the words I've grown accustomed to,

your thoughts long shadows,
blue lines and red, crossing
and recrossing on the page
bringing to life your life

behind the sheer curtains of your room
where you lie awake,
hardly aware of how swiftly
the years have gone, how the grass
at the children's feet has vanished.

In Praise of What We Have

Another day and sun breaks through.
I work in the garden early, tie back
honeysuckle. Everything I want in order
waits my attention. I think of friends
lost and present. The mountain ash
and laburnum bear blossoms.
I stand back from my work
and looking across the wall, see the child
let the wind take his kite up into the sky.

Portrait of Parents and Child

Sunday afternoon, I drive to my friend
in blinding rain. I climb the steps
to her kitchen door. The husband greets me,
their child does not look up from his game.

This boy no longer has eye-lashes or hair,
his face is pale, his mother's eyes
are vacant with grief,
her husband's eyes despair.

The child's bicycle is abandoned
in the yard; the dog slouches towards
the shed. We sit at the table,
tea is carefully poured. We talk.

Sun breaks through rain,
light enters the room. The cold sun
has travelled great distances of space,
is ignored by mother, father and child.

The spring blossoms in the mind
interweave with thoughts of pain.
This burning behind my eyes persists
and far away I hear

sounds of a train hurtling into the dark.

Remembered Time

It is the same as before in the café
with the green awning, our chairs tilted
backwards, the young waiter hovering
in the darkness behind us,
and the rain quietly falling.
Dear heart, it is remembered time
we have survived.

London in December

The air is cold between us,
a tuning fork for the words we use.

You shrug the collar of your borrowed coat.
We board a bus.
The misted window separates us
from passersby beyond
our touch, beyond our lives.

Snow turns to rain on the Thames.
I am cold to the bone,
to the very roots of my hair.

The Choice

You speak the easy language
of the happy in strange tones
yet you know what you see
when you look up and out.

But the curled-up worm inside
would have your eyes rest
on the window-sill; on mirror, clock,
jar with painted humming-birds, Fabergé egg.

Storm-clouds break and rain falls hard.

You lift your journal. The worm
writes what you write or cancels it.
Your only chance (you could take it)
would be to embrace all

rather than move on with heavy steps.

Poppies In Dominick Street

Above the rain-swept slate
streaks of light alert you again
and again to a silence
in which this place you know
is about to share some secret.

You lean against the lectern
and speak of orchards, memory,
of setting out on that journey;
how your patch of earth
transformed itself.

And I, who dreamed
of putting into words and phrases
thoughts conceived on a train
between cities or stations
amidst jarring and coupling,

listened to you
tell of your inner landscapes,
allowing you leave your sufferings
in my palm, holding them
until they became

a field of poppies, mad with light.

Knockma in Spring

Late February snow in the fields
and the Corrib a ribbon of silver
in the distance. We climb Knockma,
stopping for breath after each of the five
inclines, time and again being surprised
by the slender branches of birches, white
as girls in Communion dresses. Mulch
of dead leaves under our feet
and the velvet silence at last
when we reach the summit. A catch
in the throat, eyes smarting in the cold,
and the words we share are echoes
astonishing us in a world
that is suddenly hidden or half-seen.

White Boat In Clear Blue Water

That I thought it a mirage
was not strange, this boat so white
and light on clear blue water, tethered
to a lake-shore under Maamturk.

It was an August afternoon
sunlight followed by shadow,
one as important as the other,
as things are seen or not.

Listen, my love, I am trying
to clear a *fin-de-siècle* time
and space for you in this landscape
which breaks the heart

with its pure silence, its little boat
rocking gently, the mist on stones
sweeping like blown snow
over a world in which we are closed.

The Infinite

A version of *L'infinito* (1819) Giacomo Leopardi

Always beloved of mine, the lonely hill,
and the hedge between the horizon and my eyes.
Sitting, I look into my heart, thoughts of
eternal space beyond it,
greater silences, deep unbroken quietness,
in which I tremble, my heart afraid.
The wind is moving restlessly among the trees
and I liken that endless silence to this voice:
eternity, that which is gone, and this sound
here and alive, filling my mind. I drown
in that which is far greater than my thought:
sea, shipwreck. O beloved!

Snowberries

The year is old; more has happened
than is carried. I lean on a stone wall
and look across empty fields
in a silence broken by the menace
of wind in the trees.

In the ditch the only things
that shine are snowberries
and although almost beyond reach
I gather them with gloved hands.

Glassilaun

On a winter night I dreamed
I walked the beach at Glassilaun
when the tide had turned.

I gathered shells and stones
choosing what others passed over.

Sea-wrack rotten and brittle under my feet.
In my mouth a taste of salt
as wave upon wave, the ocean heaved.

Then I woke. It snowed outside.
A coldness in the room.

The dream that was alive is dead,
though not in memory. Wave upon wave
all the memories of my life…

This one's image stares from a photograph,
another's silk scarf is around my neck.

You are back, and you, and you…

II.
from *The Wind Beyond The Wall*

Wild Woodbine

Wild woodbine was beyond my reach
in the thick hedges round Lough Gill.
The heavy scent filled the house for days
when my father brought it in
and it stayed fresh far longer
then meadowsweet.

Because I loved the delicate
pink and white wild rose
he picked it too, cursing the thorns, muttering
"it dies too soon,
you'd be better leaving it alone".

Yet once, when my mother
swept its petals from the floor
I saw him rescue one
and place it carefully
in the small wallet
where he kept her photograph.

The Green Quilt

My mother used to say,
it's the banshee crying on the wind
from the north telling us
who has been lost at sea tonight,
until we would beg for mercy
beneath the green quilt.

At night, with the long curtains drawn,
before we could read or write,
she took us in,
the lamp dark beside the bed
and we lay still listening
to the rain ticking on the roof.

I lie awake now nights
hearing sounds the house makes
and it is her voice I remember
between the sheets,
her voice taking up right
where she had left off.

I feel her heat in the nest
she made for us
under the green quilt.

The Other Woman

Hand-washing in the kitchen
turning to watch my child,

I was a child

in another kitchen
watching
a woman weeping
into her washing

her cigarette ash
lengthening and dropping
unchecked on the clothes.

Classibawn

We tied ropes to poles on the street,
and the length of the swing
was the length of the rope.
We drew hopscotch squares there too,
and swore at the meat factory girls
who let water drip from tin buckets
spoiling the chalky game.
We were sent on walks to the Holy Well
because it used to take us ages
and my mother thought the air
and the prayers good for us.
Then one summer my father hired a Ford car
and drove us to Mullaghmore
where I saw Classibawn for the first time.
After that nothing was the same.

The Wedding Ring

In my sleep
I search in deep woods;
I am with a woman whose fingers
reach deeply into the earth.

She wears no wedding ring
for she has lost it in the undergrowth.
Her other children have climbed trees
and are throwing scaldings from their nests.

As thunder mounts behind us,
trucks of cattle roar past,
their faces pressed close
to slats for air.

I see my mother, her hands
in wet dirt, searching,
searching for her ring among pine needles
and the blood of young birds.

My Father

My father
was a lonely man
whose fifty years
at sea
had left
no deeper blue
in his eyes.

Once in spring
at Lissadell
he picked bluebells
for my mother
and his eyes
looked different.

He fought
death
a frightened man,
hauled
to unknown rocks
from an ocean
he could
not navigate.

I wonder nights now
what lonely bay
he sails in
and does he
quote his lines of Yeats
and smoke his pipe
and drink the whiskey
for the pain.

The Broken Swing

Come with me
through the rusting gates
from the streets of the town
into this high-walled garden
and move ankle deep in bluebells
under the beech trees
where the bickering crows
nest high.

Come through the storm door
to the shadows of the house
and when your eyes grow used to the dim light
step over the old papers, the clothes
piled up on the chairs and draw close
to the black and white photograph
of your mother. Be quiet
and you might even hear the piano played.

Show me the bedroom where you slept,
your toys still on the floor.
Shake the dust from the books
you had forgotten about
and I will follow you then
to the garden with the broken swing.

Mend it quickly and bring
your children here.

Take them in from the town
to pick bluebells in the garden.
Stay near the house with the shuttered windows
from where you first saw the stars.

Culleenamore

I wish that before we left that place
I had told you the story
of how the Atlantic salt-waters'
taste in my mouth
leaves me loneliest.

It was that kind of Sunday afternoon
in Culleenamore,
a wind through the bent grass and sandhills
making me want to begin
a history of my past,
every chapter unfolding

pictures of a man
lying under a hawthorn, reading,
his jacket bundled into a pillow,
a woman straining her ears
hard to hear the voices
of a boy and his sisters

disappearing into the perilous water.

The Wind Beyond The Wall

The wind beyond the high wall
at the back of our house
contained itself there,
when barefoot, on the cold bedroom floor
I pressed my face against the glass.

Curtains billowed back created
swaying shadows in the small room.
The night was another world
and I was safe, apart
from the wind beyond the wall.

The lamp before the Sacred Heart glowed,
coals hissed in the grate
and on days missed from school
the hands of the clock on the mantelpiece
seemed scarcely to move at all.

On the small round table
she set cups, plates, new bread.
Mice scuttled in the skirting
when she softly dusted the photograph
of the man in uniform.

In dreams I see his face, recognize
his penetrating gaze
and she and I are back in that house
wanting something beyond
my touch, beyond hers.

Primroses In March

I placed them in the earthenware jug, asking,
"what do they remind you of?"
The question hung in the air
while I floated for a moment on a breeze
that crossed his face.

I thought of Sligo lanes and primroses
clawed from moss beneath trees,
taking them home
to my mother, filling her lap
with damp stems, their broken heads.

Earlier that day
I pulled these frail ones
to ease a particular hunger of my own,
later wishing I had left them
where they had grown.

From that bleak headland
I took primroses for free,
the mist from Lough Corrib
biting to the bone
through the thin lilac dress I wore.

March hailstones hit
against the window pane
and we talked on lightly
as if the sun still shone
on the fragile flowers between us.

Martha

Martha, finding shade beneath
laburnums, remembered the market,
how women laughed at her extravagance,
a pound of costly perfume,
pure oils, best grain
for bread.

Lazarus, her brother
who entered death,
walked once more between trees
and she caught his eyes in detail
and delight.

Martha, weaving in silence, grew cold.

She who trembled when His name, their guest,
"The Nazarene" was first raised
on the wind around Jerusalem,
found she asked
for more.

She who built fires, baked bread,
uncovered their good ware,
filled the house with light
and sweet flowers, now
drew her thin cloak about her
and wept.

Even the birds were still. Martha
caught the scent of perfume
in the garden as evening
turned to night.

The Master was with her sister, Mary.

She was wiping His feet
with her hair.

This Moon, These Stars

Something is changing.
There is a September stillness in the garden.

We have woken in this bed for years.
You have followed me into my poems,
my dreams, my past, to places I scarcely
know of myself.

I called one evening
from our back doorstep. "Look," I said,
"look at this moon." We stood there
in silence, not touching, not knowing
what to say.

We have been together many days, many nights.
These stars have come out
over us again and again.

Here is the life we are living,
not on a windswept beach, not in vast
city streets, not in a strange country
but here, where we have chosen to be.

I look at myself in the glass, at the woman
I am.

I think of our days, our years running on
into each other.

What will we say,
what will we know.
Separate, together,
will we find the right way, the dream
neither of us can explain.

I pull the living room curtains together.
The garden is around us,
still above us are the stars,
light and indestructible.

Poem For St. Brigid's Day

I

Children gather rushes,
wind whistles through their fingers,
rain blurs their vision;
all evening they will weave
and interweave crosses,
the history of Brigid's love.

II

It is early morning. A chieftain
slowly lifts his head, sees a woman enter
bearing armfuls of green spokes.
Her face floats
all day about him, her body's outline
vague.

He woke twice that night,
wandered to the window
tired with darkness,
unaware what had bound them
together; spring, perhaps,
the green stems,

her breath warm
on his face or their two shadows
caught in branches outside
like fish in a net.

The Straw Hat

Some things insist on becoming lost,
like the be-ribboned straw hat
the girl waved over the bridge
to me.

How ridiculous it looked,
floating on the water
between two swans
who were coaxing
one another to love.

Although I tried to reach it,
it was swept away.
"Sit still in the boat, you fool,"
she called, "sit still
or you'll fall into the river."

Inis Meáin

Who, seeing me, knows I walked
through fields of corn
and, with you, once heard
the lost curlew mourn
when even north winds were delicate;
I reach this place over and over,
retrace my steps from Cill Cheannach
to Dún Chonchuir despite the roughness of stone.

For I need the sound the high wind makes
in the dry grass, the old and low
notes of island melody, sung at night
when summer is almost ended; and the silence,
full as rains falling after Sunday Mass
on the fringes of island women's shawls.

III.
from *A Walled Garden In Moylough*

Rose Cottage, Finisklin, c1955

I am peeling potatoes for dinner, thinking
about this and that, a sun-filled orchard,
my mother and her friend under laburnums.

My mother's friend is washing in the old style,
wash, wash, wring, rinse
like her mother and her grandmother.

In a barrel of rainwater near the kitchen
window-sill, her daughter washes her feet
while I whisper in the trees with my sister.

Thirty years from then my mother sits
with old photographs, wearing night clothes all day,
remembers liking jazz, faded films, Fred Astaire;

thinks of children in an apple orchard
and waits in silence for someone
to touch in passing an old woman's hair.

The Nest

I

At dusk we found it in the hedge,
four eggs like tiny speckled
marbles, still warm
when we held them in the palm
of our hands.

I threw one down, then another.

You laughed. I threw one more.
You passed me back the last to throw.

Splinters of shell, feathers, blood,
a yellow streaked-with-green mess
lay in the middle of the tarred road.

We ran home through dark fields,
crossed gates.

All night I sucked my fingers.
A full moon outside my window
sat in a cold sky.

II

I sit here
in a half-lit room,
a black stain at my heart.

I am on an empty road.
The ditch is wrapped
in its own shadows,
a nest is full of bits of white down.

A Walled Garden in Moylough

Now this May evening is quietly breathing
around us; your tobacco smoke swirls
in the stillness and I remember my lost father.

The wide street outside is silent.
Houses, shops and church are shuttered
and a light rain drifts in from farms and quiet fields.

The story begins: we are attentive to one another
knowing what we already know will be transformed
as a baby on its way transforms the young mother.

The evening darkens. The words we share lift clearly.

Inside our glasses are cooling on a low table.
In firelight we yearn for something nameless,
freely given as trees, meadows and frail bluebells.

I stand at the window. The garden's lunar shadows
fall on white stone and juniper, and I know
my stillness is part of yours in the walled garden.

Someone Should Tell My Mother

Tonight my mother is walking in a bare room
over my head.

Someone should tell her to sleep now.

Tonight my mother is holding a skirt-full
of apples warm against her breast.

Someone should tell her to eat now.

Tonight my mother is sewing a dress for me.
She cries out when the needle pierces her hand.

Someone should tell her how helpless I am.

Tonight I will tell my mother she must
leave me alone, but wait, I cannot.

I hear a rustling sound coming from the room

like someone sifting through hundreds of pages
seeking a happy ending and the sound is like the sea

which is very far away.

Bog-Cotton

The fields are drenched with it,
feather-down heads, gossamer
on stalks both hardy and frail.
Nothing breaks the silence
in a Roundstone bog
but a curlew's cry caught in the wind.

The mist clears; I pass a woman
standing on a grass verge,
smiling, talking to herself.
Wet grass anoints her ankles,
her voice falters, drifts.

Behind a wall horses grow restless,
seagulls clamour overhead
and the woman is silent,
I walk to the end of Inishnee
where shadows fall on rocks and shore

and the sun shines on *ceannabhán*,
mysterious, *uaigneach*.

The Mountain Ash

If you can imagine it
fully grown, red berries
in clusters on every branch,
and if you understand
my desire to tend it
always in my own place,
you will know why I carried
it here as a sapling,
uncovered the roots from plastic,
exposed them to the cold air.

This sheltered garden
will never resemble
its wild hills nor the soil
deceive as black earth
of the mountain, yet
I can be seduced into believing
my mountain ash
will live, and day after day
draw me to the window,
allow me rise with certainty.

I carry my washing in and out
in great armfuls,
bring a necessary stake
to my mountain ash when it struggles
against the harsher winds.

Blind with sleet, on days I cannot
see my face in the mirror
it comforts me as neither child
nor lover could. I planted it.
Without me it will die.

The Little Street

(after Vermeer, Rijksmuseum, Amsterdam)

I

She is sitting with her sewing in an open door,
the dark behind her.

Although the little street is quiet and still,
she is not alone.

The girl-child she watches over
plays with her dog, motionless in the heat

and her friend, sister or neighbour
washes her hands in the rain barrel.

All are in their own light and shadow.
There is no speech between them.

(My shadows have returned, encircling me
in this space. I turn away).

II

My grandmother, wearing black, is sitting
on a kitchen chair outside our front door.

My mother is standing at the stove, wiping
tears from her eyes, about to call out.

I am wearing no shoes. It is summer
and there are daisies in the wet grass.

And now as I remember it, a man
is stumbling down the little street,

squinting in the sun, saying something
we can almost hear. We have all turned away.

In the Brief Time Given

I stand by the table, making rules
for my child, his hand on the fruit,
his eyes looking beyond me through the window
at the trees and the bird tuning up.

I tell him not to put shoes on the table,
bring hawthorn indoors, break mirrors
or open umbrellas in the house.

Rain pours on lilacs in the yard
and I shelter him with myself.
Then I get on with the morning wash,
the child leaving me to it, taking with him
into the distance images of secret and threat,
alive to what my words said
and did not say, in the brief time given.

On Hearing My Daughter
Play "The Swan"

My daughter plays Saint-Saëns. It is evening
and spring. Suddenly I am outside
a half-opened door. I am six years old
but I already know there's a kind
of music that can destroy.

My mother is playing a waltz, Chopin,
and everything is possible. There are lilacs
in a vase on the hall table, white among
the colourful umbrellas, folded,
full of the morning's light rain.

My sisters' voices are calling one another
far down the street. There are wind-blown leaves
under my father's feet as he enters the room.
I look at him as if for the first time
and he grows old.

I see my mother rise from the piano
and close it gently. She takes a glass
from the table. It is empty. But she has put
a weight in me, the weight of something
that has died in her.

As my daughter sustains the melody
with her right hand, the tumult
of the chords she uses with her left hand
brings into the room
the hush and roar of the sea.

The Photograph of My Aunts

The photograph I found beneath the purple box
must have been lost and left behind.
It shows two sisters wearing white lace
in late summertime.

Goats graze under lilac trees. Two older women
wearing straw hats, stitch in pink and blue,
tiny knitted garments; their dresses blow in a breeze
that lifts the edges, revealing black button boots.

The sisters near the window–frame
have hair blown in a hazy lane.
This portrait stares from my wall,
the faces haunt me with other likenesses.

It hangs over the piano
near the painting of an apple orchard.
The sisters are dead.
In the photograph they wear white shoes.

They lean against the warm wall of the house.

Woman Herding Cattle
in a Field near Kilcolgan

Whenever I see her
in my mind's eye
I see her squat body in a crossover apron
and boots, calmly walking her field.

The spring night has come on,
taken me unawares and the lane is dark out there.
I think of her alone beside the hearth,
the radio turned on.

Whenever bare branches
turn again to leaf,
I will remember her
walking quietly in a sunlit space.

I will think of the woman
herding cattle in a field near Kilcolgan
alive with herself, company
for sheep and cows.

When I wake in the night
I see her too, young
and light-haired,
running in a green field.

Veronica

I

Veronica's maidservant scrubs the floor.

Her washing heavy on her hip, Veronica
goes to the river where singing women
beat hempen clothes on stones.

Plunging her hands into cold water,
watching them redden, grow coarse,
she remembers once being told death
by drowning is like strangulation.

Noon, and a dead cat lies sprawled
in the dust.

Finished her chores, the maidservant
lurking in shadows hides her face beneath lace.

Veronica lingers by the river, dreaming
of March in the garden, the hard hot earth,
smell of oranges and grass.

II

Her kitchen is dim. Herbs dangle
from the rafters, copper pans on the walls
are campfires in candlelight.

The maidservant is threading a needle
with grey-blue wool.
Veronica is at the table, her floury hands
knead dough.

It is not this she thinks about, but the outline
of a face on white cloth, the way it moved
in the breeze when she hung it
on the clothesline in the garden,

how it caressed her arms.

On Reading Your Letter in June

June and the hedges are drenched with hawthorn.
It is evening. There is a silken rustle
in the beeches. I sit with your letter; the wind makes
the whispering sound of lovers' laughter;

laughing I wore a blue dress at the water's edge,
your fingers stretched out to touch me. Nothing
kept me from you. In the morning there was
lavender on the window-sill and to this I return;

returning each time to find it startles like something
that is itself. Nearly midnight, I stand
in the open doorway. I speak to you
but your back is turned. You are painting a picture;

picturing a stone cottage, alone and exposed.
Two people have arrived from another place.
Over a bridge. You have painted trees the colour of rust.
You sign the painting with your name,

your name that no longer catches in my throat.
Look at you wrapping yourself up in your dark coat.
See how the trees have darkened. The town lights
have come on and each house holds a woman.

The two in the painting survive. I finish your letter.

Hanging Wallpaper

It has gone on all morning.
Scrape, scrape, tear, strip,
the sound is in my head,

I am clenching my teeth,
it is inside my belly
until I cannot bear it any longer.

I am in a room
on the other side of the wall.
I stretch my legs out under a table.

They feel like someone else's
excavated from a pit.
But wait. The scraping has ceased.

Frost in the garden, half-starved birds,
dead flowers. The leaves are falling,
the old wallpaper is falling.

Time to hang the new,
choose the colour quickly – pink, blue?

The Iris Garden

High over the harbour
we are in the iris garden;
all the others are in the glass room
bending towards one another.

We speak of how soon
you will be with us
not raising our voices above
a whisper; you are the breath between us.

Our blue dresses move gently.
There are only two irises
open to the sun and they lean
against a wall, are naked.

Our eyes are shut but not sleeping.
We tell each other how little
we remember even when we were awake
and it was morning.

The sea is groaning down below,
ebbing, flowing and carrying
its wrack to the shore; we know
and we imagine you there, almost.

Fionnuala

Imagine the bell's call
in a town asleep
beneath bleak mountains,

a woman alone in a room,
a vase with blossoms,
scentless things.

The dark sky
shadows a space,
the white page,

rage of winter
in the alders
and Lir's daughter,

a swan in waters
wilder, deeper
than she's ever known,

laments and laments again.

Winding the Wool

She unplaited the figure-of-eight shape
of the skein and stretched it wide
apart, suddenly taut in her arms.

She placed it over my small upturned hands
and we sat face to face,
while she started to wind it in a ball.

Wool moved from here to there, the thread
running from my fingers quickly,
like rain streaming on the window pane.

The final inches slipped away from me
and she dropped her newly wound ball
on the floor. She worked the end
taken from me into her first stitches.

Hands still in my lap, I sat on a wicker
chair. Shadows from the fire
danced strangely on the wall
behind her head. I watched the thread.

The Lost Brooch

Newport, Co. Mayo, August 1993.

As I remember it,
there were oak trees
on both sides of a gravel
path, the stones were wet.

We had not sought shelter,
only tea and talk
in Newport House,
its windows open, beckoning.

There was no such welcome,
being a festival day
in the small town, visitors
of all kind around.

Through stalls and barrows,
oysters, balloons and painted faces,
we wove a steady path,
found a coffee shop and then

you entered with your friend
whose name, Hazel, reminded me
of childhood, a lake,
a wood, my white bicycle, plain bread.

"And what is it you've lost?"
I eyed you warily and reached
across my breast, my gaze
never leaving your face.

You held it out to me
in all its round, moon-gold glory,
the hooped brooch bought in Amsterdam,
a lover's gift, a pledge.

I took it from you, examined
the weakened pin. Sunlight
filled the place, encircled us.
We drank our tea, later wine

and time became an acorn
in a green case, floating
on a river in full flood
rising, falling before our eyes.

One for Sorrow

One magpie rests on a winter bush.
Crows scavenge a stubble field.

From where I am I cannot see or hear you.
The train moves west. You disappear.
Yet the wool I feel beneath my fingers
is the wool of your coat.

You stood outside the door,
shaded your eyes and said
"the blackbird, it's the blackbird I hear!"

Notes and Dedications

The epigraph on Page 4 is taken from a poem by Carolyn Forché, "Because One Is Always Forgotten", i.m. José Rudolfo Viera 1939-1981: El Salvador. Published in *The Country Between Us* (London, Jonathan Cape, 1983).

The epigraph on Page 7 is taken from a poem by Anne Kennedy, "Burial Instructions". Published in *The Dog Kubla Dreams My Life* (Galway, Salmon Publishing, 1994).

"Classibawn" on Page 40 is from the Irish, "caisleán bán" which means "white castle". It is the name given to a castle residence situated in Mullaghmore, County Sligo.

St. Brigid in "Poem for St. Brigid's Day", Page 49, is the patroness of Ireland; called in Irish "Muire na nGael" or "Mary of the Gaels". Her Feast day falls on February 1st and is traditionally observed in Ireland by the making of rush crosses.

"Inis Meáin", Page 51, is the middle island of the three Aran Islands situated off the coast of County Galway, Ireland. Cill Cheannach refers to the monastic remains of a church on the island. Tradition identifies Cill Cheannach (Kilcanagh) with St. Gregory who gives his name to the Sound between the islands. Dún Chonchuir is the largest noble fort remains on the islands of Aran. Also called "Dún Conor".

In the poem "Bog-Cotton", Page 71, the Irish word *ceannabhán* means bog-cotton and the Irish word *uaigneach* means lonely.

Further Acknowledgements

Acknowledgement is made to the editors of the publications in which some of the poems from THE WIND BEYOND THE WALL first appeared: *The Tuam Herald; Writing in the West* (The Connacht Tribune)*; The Salmon; Krino; Cyphers; Poetry Ireland Review; New Irish Writing (The Sunday Tribune); The Maryland Review* (U.S.)*; Visions* (U.S.)*; The Cork Yule Book; The Honest Ulsterman; The Simon Poetry Anthology; The Dundalk Poetry Anthology;, Anima; Riverine; Limerick Poetry Broadsheet*; and *W.E.B.* (New Irish Writing by Women).

Acknowledgements are also due to the editors of the publications in which some of the poems from A WALLED GARDEN IN MOYLOUGH first appeared: *Poetry Ireland Review; The Salmon; Cyphers; Fortnight; The Honest Ulsterman; The Applegarth Review; Force 10; Colby Quarterly* Vol. 28, No.4*; Riverine; La Collina Anno* VIII/IX, Numero 16/18 (Italy)*; Woman's Way; The Sligo Champion; Writing in The West* (Connacht Tribune)*; The Tuam Herald; The Great Tuam Annual; The Fiddlehead* (Canada)*; Grain (Canada); Irish America; Westerly* (Australia)*; Verse (Scotland); The Great Book of Ireland; The Mayo Anthology; The Humours of Galway; The Inward Eye* (Sligo Poetry Broadsheet)*; Women's Work* (Wexford)*; Under the Shadow − Westport Poetry Anthology; Irish Poetry Now − Other Voices; The Poet and the World − International Poetry Anthology* (Seattle, U.S.A.)*; Cúirt Anthology* No.1*; Full Moon* (Killybegs Poetry Broadsheet)*; U.C.G. Women's Studies Review* Vol.I, Vol.II*; Seneca Review* (U.S.A.) Vol.23, Nos.1&2 − (Special Issue, *Irish Women Poets*)*; The Southern Review* (U.S.A.)*; The Maryland Poetry Review* (U.S.A.)*; Ms. Chief; Irish Women's Review; Lifelines; Real Cool: Poems to Grow Up With*; and *Mná na hEorpa* Broadsheet (International Women's Day 1993).

About the Author

JOAN McBREEN is from Sligo; she now lives in Tuam, County Galway. Her poetry collections are *The Wind Beyond the Wall* (Story Line Press, Oregon, 1990; reprinted 1991) and *A Walled Garden in Moylough* (Story Line Press and Salmon Publishing, Galway, 1995). In 1997 she was awarded an MA in Women's Studies by University College, Dublin, presenting A Dictionary of Twentieth-Century Irish Women Poets as her dissertation. Her poetry is published widely in Ireland and abroad and has been broadcast, anthologised and translated into many languages. Her anthology *The White Page/An Bhileog Bhán – Twentieth Century Irish Women Poets* was published by Salmon Publishing in 1999 (reprinted 2000, 2001).